Bryan Willis

RACING RULES 2025-2028 COMPANION

FERNHURST BOOKS

PLAYING THE GAME

Racing sailors are on trust to play the game of sailing fairly, and comply with the racing rules. When you accidentally break a rule and you are not exonerated, you must take a penalty.

Cheating, lying in a hearing, or playing the game unfairly can be penalized severely. If you feel you must cheat, please take up another sport.

BASIC PRINCIPLE:
'Sportsmanship and the Rules'
RULE 2

HELPING THOSE IN DANGER

You must help any person or vessel in danger. You can be compensated with points for the position in which you would have finished.

RULE 1.1

PROPULSION

With some exceptions, you must use only the wind and water to increase, maintain, or decrease your boat's speed. You may adjust the trim of sails and hull, and perform other acts of seamanship, but must not otherwise move your body to propel the boat.

Three of the exceptions are:

(a) You may move your body to exaggerate the rolling that helps the boat through a tack or a gybe, provided that, immediately afterwards, your boat's speed is not greater than it would have been in the absence of the tack or gybe.

(b) When surfing (rapidly accelerating down the front of a wave), or planing is possible, the crew may pull the sheet and the guy of any sail in order to **initiate** surfing or planing, but only **once** for each wave or gust of wind. When foiling is possible, each sail may be pulled in any number of times to initiate foiling. No pumps are permitted to **maintain** surfing, planing, or foiling.

(c) If a batten is inverted, provided it does not clearly propel the boat, you may pump the sail until the batten is no longer inverted.

RULE 42

CREW POSITION, LIFELINES

Your crew may use toestraps if class rules permit them, but you mustn't rig other hiking devices. If your boat has lifelines then, other than to perform temporary tasks, the crew's torsos must stay inside the lower lifeline.

RULE 49

RACING v CRUISING

Boats that are not racing or intending to race are governed by the Collision Regulations (also known as 'ColRegs', International Regulations for Preventing Collisions at Sea, or IRPCAS).

Between a boat that is racing and one that is not, the Collision Regulations apply. Racing boats have no special rights over cruising or commercial vessels.

All boats, whether or not they are racing, are required by the Collision Regulations not to obstruct vessels that have restricted manoeuvrability. Other local regulations may also apply.

RULE Part 2 Preamble

EVENT ORGANIZATION

The Organizing Authority publishes a Notice of Race on which you decide whether or not to enter the race or series. If you enter, the Race Committee must provide you with Sailing Instructions which will include a description of the marks, the starting and finishing lines, and the course to be sailed. The Race Committee runs the races and produces the results.

RULES 89.2 & 90

WHEN BOATS MEET

When two boats meet, one is the KEEP-CLEAR boat and the other is the RIGHT-of-WAY boat. The right-of-way boat may sail any course but always has some obligations. If she changes course she must give the other boat room to keep clear. She must always try to avoid contact, and sometimes she is required to 'give room' or 'give mark-room' or 'not sail above her proper course'.

RULES OF PART 2
Definitions

3. BASIC PRINCIPLES

BEFORE THE START

Your boat must be afloat and off moorings at the preparatory signal.

RULE 45

MAKING FAST; ANCHORING

After the preparatory signal, you mustn't make fast (tie up) except to bail, reef sails, or make repairs. You may anchor but must recover the anchor if possible.

RULE 45

STARTING

At the starting signal, the hull of your boat must be completely on the pre-start side of the starting line. If it is not, you must sail to the pre-start side, keeping clear of boats that have started correctly.

RULE 21.1 & Definition Start

SAILING THE COURSE

You must sail the course, which means start, round or pass the marks as described in the sailing instructions, and finish. A string representing your boat's track from when you begin to approach the starting line to start until you finish must, when drawn taut, pass each mark on the required side and in the correct order, touch each rounding mark, and pass between the marks of a gate from the direction of the previous mark. You may correct any errors to comply with this rule provided you have not finished.

Definition Sail the Course

FINISHING

You finish when any part of your hull touches the finishing line from the course side, but not if you thereafter take a penalty, correct an error in sailing the course made at the line, or continue to sail the course.

RULE 28
Definition Finish

ON A TACK

A boat is on the tack, starboard or port, corresponding to her windward side (usually the opposite side to the sail).

The yellow boats are on port tack, the blue boats are on starboard tack (even with the sail pushed to windward).

LEEWARD AND WINDWARD

When two boats on the same tack overlap, the one on the leeward side of the other is the leeward boat. The other is the windward boat.

The yellow boats are to windward of the respective blue boats.

OVERLAP, CLEAR AHEAD, CLEAR ASTERN

Rights and obligations often change when boats become overlapped, or an overlap is broken. The bits of the boat that count for overlaps are 'hull and equipment in normal position', so a bowsprit would count if it is in its normal position at the time.

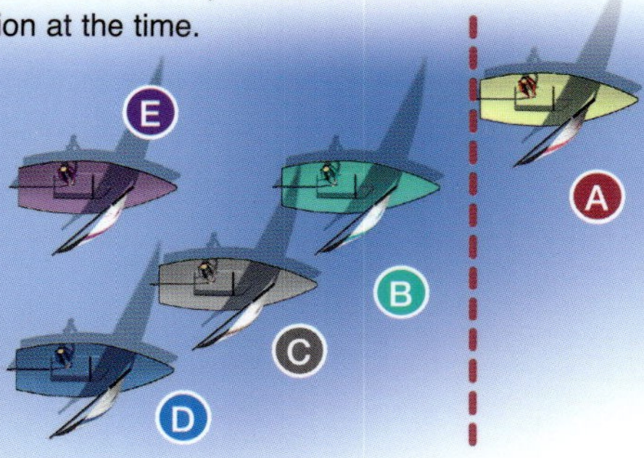

A is clear ahead of all the others. B & C are overlapped. C & D are overlapped. B & D are overlapped because C is between them. B & E are not overlapped because C is not between them.

6. KEEPING CLEAR

A keep-clear boat keeps clear of a right-of-way boat if the right-of-way boat can sail her course with no need to take avoiding action and, when the boats are *overlapped* (both on the same tack or both sailing downwind), if the right-of-way boat can change course in both directions without immediately making contact with the keep-clear boat.

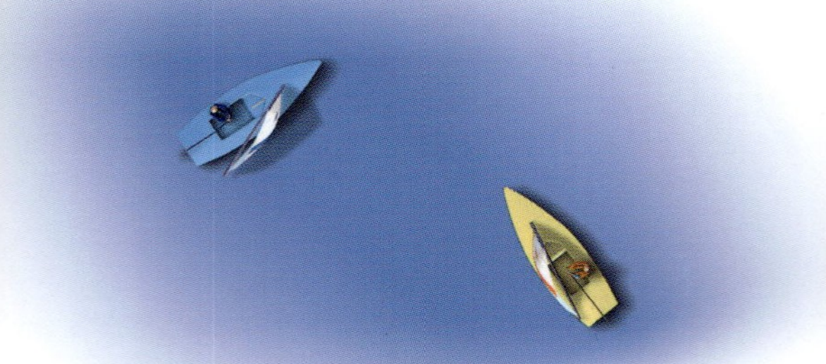

If Yellow can sail her course without the need to take avoiding action, then Blue is keeping clear.

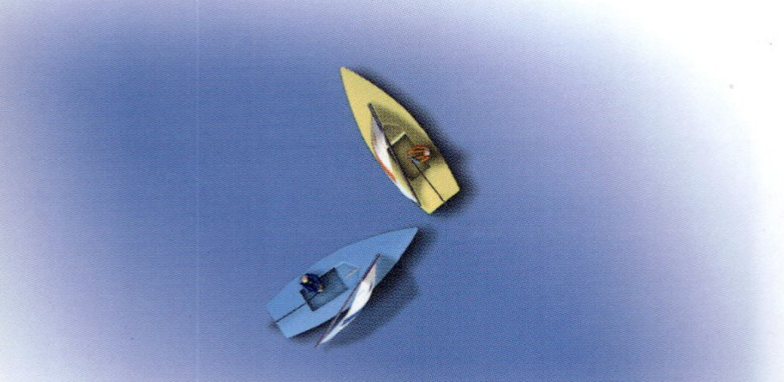

Blue ducks under Yellow's stern. If these are dinghies on flat water and there is no contact, Blue has kept clear. If they are keelboats in strong winds and high seas, Yellow would be justified in needing to change course because Blue is too close, so Blue has not kept clear.

Blue can sail her course without the need to alter course, but she cannot change course without immediately making contact with Yellow, so Yellow is not keeping clear.

Definition Keep Clear

PROPER COURSE

A boat's proper course is any course the skipper might reasonably choose so as to sail the course as quickly as possible in the absence of the nearby boat. It can take account of tidal streams, windy and windless areas, and groups of boats (but not the other boat(s) affected). In waves, a proper course may take account of crests and valleys.

A boat is never required to ***sail*** her proper course, but when a leeward boat of two or more overlapping boats established the overlap from clear astern, then she is not allowed to sail ***above*** her proper course.

A boat has no proper course before her starting signal, so the rule (below) requiring a boat not to sail above her proper course doesn't apply before the starting signal.

Definition & RULE 17

OBLIGATIONS WHEN BOATS ON THE SAME TACK ARE OVERLAPPED

A leeward boat that establishes an overlap from clear astern within two of her hull lengths of another boat, must not sail above her proper course while they are overlapped on the same tack within two hull lengths. If the overlap was established in any other way (for example, if the windward boat established the overlap to windward of the leeward boat, or the leeward boat tacked or gybed into the overlapped position) then there is no proper course restriction. But if the leeward boat luffs, she must give room to the windward boat to keep clear.

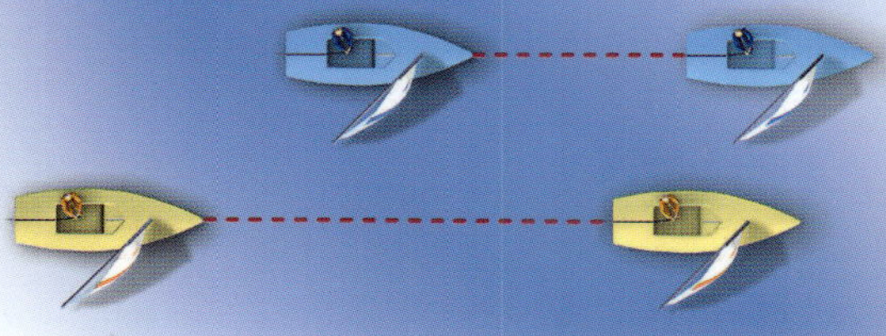

When they are overlapped Blue must keep clear. Yellow must not sail above her proper course because she established the overlap from clear astern.

RULE 17

8. BASIC RULES

ON OPPOSITE TACKS

The port-tack boat must keep clear.

The blue boats must keep clear.

RULE 10

ON THE SAME TACK

The boat clear astern (if not overlapped) or to windward (if overlapped) must keep clear.

The blue boats must keep clear.

RULES 11 & 12

ACQUIRING RIGHT OF WAY

When a boat acquires right of way, she must initially give the other boat room to keep clear (unless she acquires right of way because of the other boat's actions).

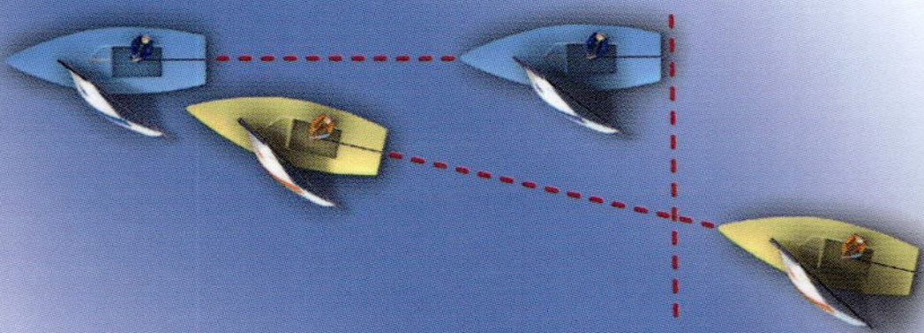

Yellow must initially give room to Blue. Blue does not need to anticipate Yellow becoming the right-of-way boat. Here Yellow has not 'initially given room', and breaks rule 15.

RULE 15

TACKING

After a boat passes head to wind, she must keep clear of other boats until she is on a close-hauled course. If she tacks into a right-of-way position, she must initially give the other boat room to keep clear.

At position 2, Yellow is on starboard tack but must keep clear till she completes the tack.

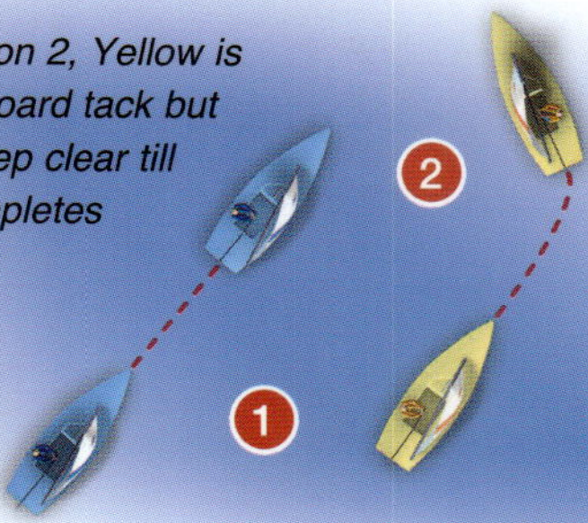

RULES 13 & 15

TACKING CLOSE (THE 'SLAM DUNK')

Blue must keep clear throughout this whole manoeuvre. If Yellow is overlapped at the moment Blue passes head-to-wind, then Yellow may luff.

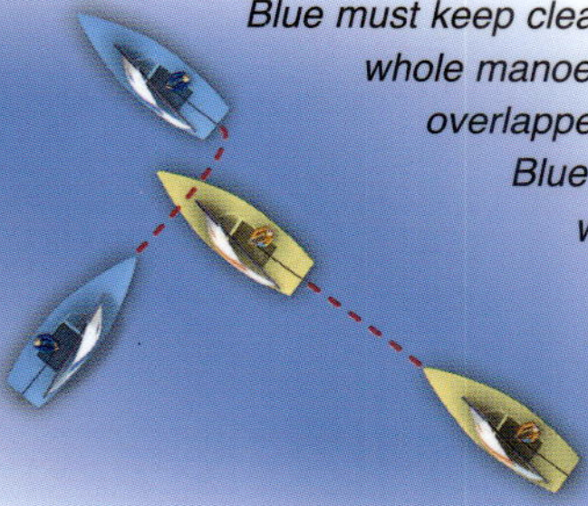

RULES 10, 13, 15, 17 & 11

TACKING CLOSE (THE 'LEE BOW')

Blue must keep clear until she completes her tack, when she becomes the right-of-way boat, but Blue must then initially give Yellow room to keep clear.

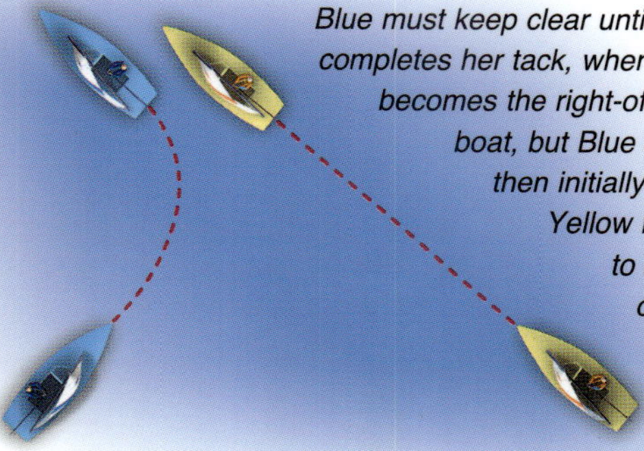

RULES 10, 13, 15 & 11

10. CHANGING COURSE

When a right-of-way boat changes course, she must usually give room to the keep-clear boat to keep clear and sometimes to round a mark. 'Room' is 'the space a boat needs in the existing conditions… while manoeuvring promptly in a seamanlike way'.

Blue must keep clear.

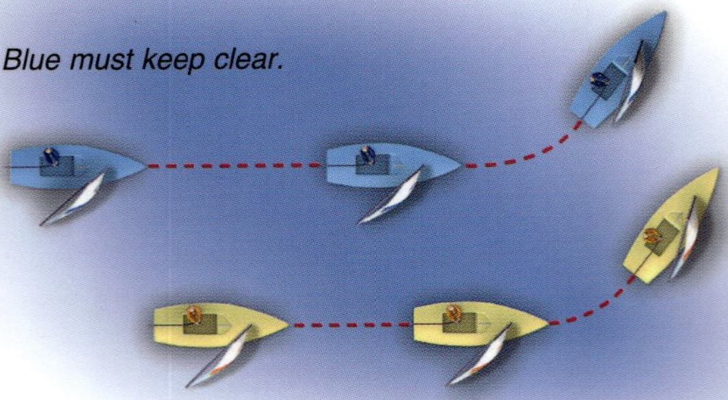

Yellow must give room to Blue to keep clear.

RULE 16.1

CHANGING COURSE ON THE BEAT

After the starting signal when boats are on a beat and P is bearing away to avoid S, S must not change course if as a result P would immediately need to change course to continue keeping clear.

Yellow bears away to pass to leeward of Blue, but because Blue changes course, Yellow needs to change her course immediately to continue keeping clear. Therefore, Blue breaks rule 16.2.

RULE 16.2

CHANGING COURSE AT A MARK

When an inside boat with right to mark-room is changing course to round the mark as necessary to sail the course, she will be exonerated if she breaks a 'when boats meet' rule, or is compelled to touch the mark.

RULE 43

AVOIDING CONTACT

If reasonably possible, a boat must avoid contact with another boat and avoid causing other boats to contact each other or an object. However, a right-of-way boat (or one entitled to room or mark-room) need not act to avoid contact until it is clear that the other boat is not keeping clear or giving room, and shall be exonerated if she breaks this rule as long as the contact causes no damage or injury.

Blue must keep clear. Both boats must try to avoid contact; however, Yellow's luff is unlikely to cause damage, and if there is no damage, Yellow will be exonerated for not avoiding contact. She might be penalized for not giving room when she changes course, but in this case the diagram shows Blue was given room but failed to keep clear.

RULES 14, 11, 16.1 & 43

Blue must keep clear and avoid contact. Yellow must try to avoid contact.

RULES 14 & 10

Here Yellow must rely on Blue's judgement. If there is contact and damage, only Blue can be penalized.

RULES 14 & 10

12. ON THE START LINE

WINDWARD AND LEEWARD

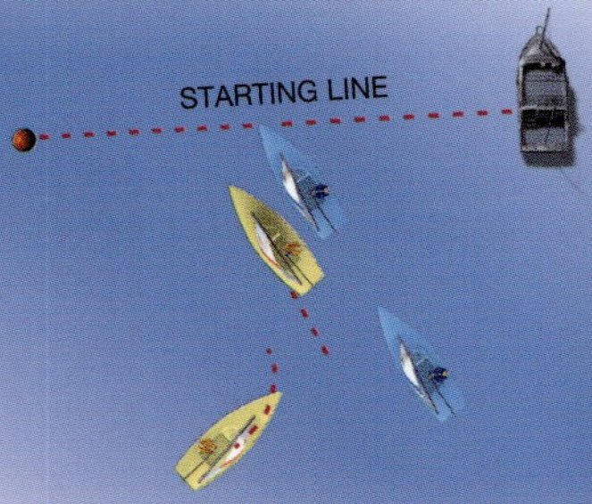

Blue is to windward and must keep clear. Yellow may change course (giving room to Blue to keep clear) even if doing so forces Blue over the starting line.

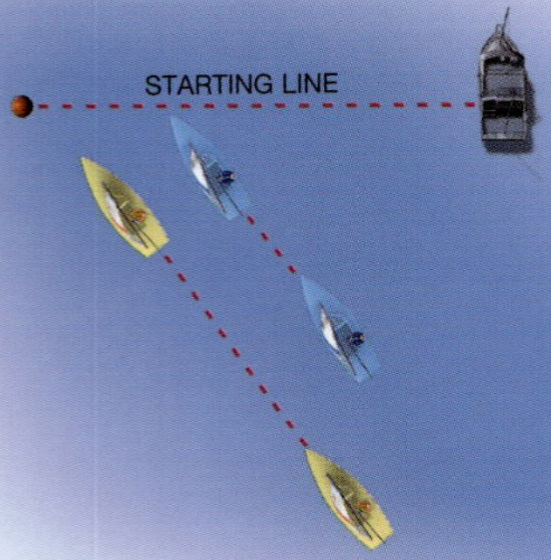

Provided the race hasn't started, Yellow may change course (giving room to Blue to keep clear) even if that forces Blue over the starting line, but once the start signal is made, because she got the overlap from clear astern, Yellow must immediately bear away to a close-hauled course (unless she needs to sail above close-hauled to get round the pin).

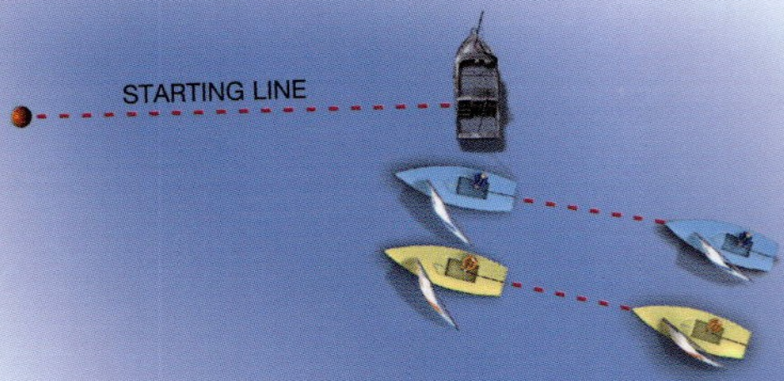

Yellow can luff (but must give room to Blue to keep clear). In the first position, if Yellow were to luff, Blue can keep clear by sailing the 'wrong side' of the committee boat, so that is what she must do if Yellow luffs. But at the second position, if Yellow luffs then Blue does not have room to keep clear, so Yellow must give Blue room to pass under the Committee Boat.

RULES 11, 15, 16.1 & 17

ON OPPOSITE TACKS AT A WINDWARD MARK

When boats are on opposite tacks, the basic rule applies: the port-tack boat must keep clear. When a boat passes head to wind inside the 'zone' (three lengths from the mark), and is then on the same tack as a boat that is fetching the mark on starboard tack, she mustn't force that boat to sail above close-hauled to avoid contact, and if the boat gets an inside overlap, the tacking boat must give mark-room.

Yellow must keep clear.

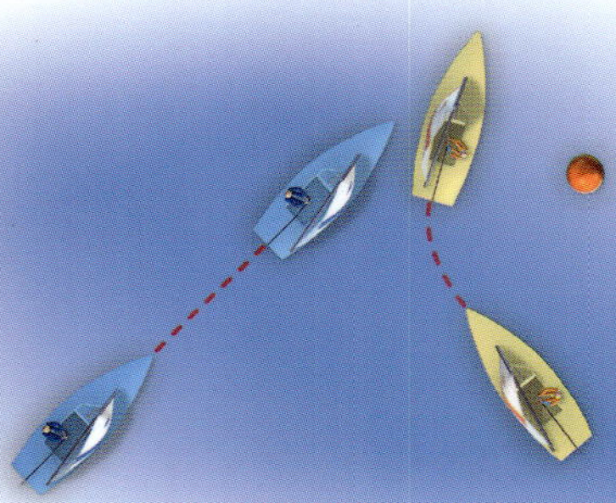

Yellow must keep clear while tacking.

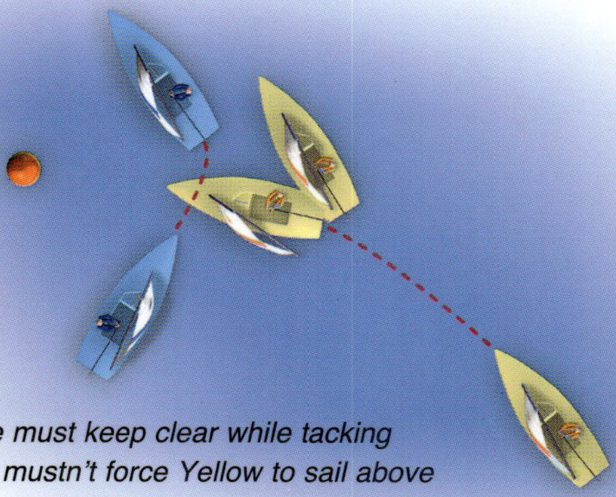

Blue must keep clear while tacking and mustn't force Yellow to sail above close-hauled to avoid contact, and if Yellow gets an inside overlap Blue must give her mark-room.

RULES 18.1 & 18.3

ROOM AT A MARK

When boats are overlapped at a mark when one boat enters the zone, the outside boat must give the inside boat 'mark-room', that is, room to sail to the mark, and round or pass it (including room to gybe if the inside boat is gybing to sail her proper course). If the inside boat has right-of-way, the outside boat must also keep clear. As long as the boat entitled to mark-room does not pass head to wind or leave the zone during the rounding, the obligation to give room continues to apply even if the overlap is broken or right-of-way changes. The obligation to give mark-room ceases to apply once the boat entitled to mark-room has been given mark-room.

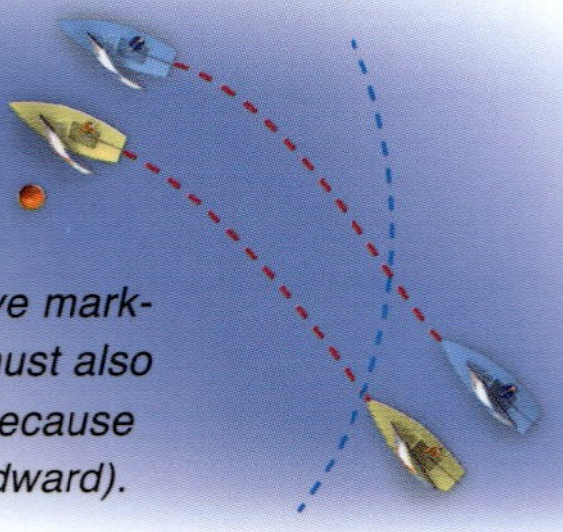

Blue must give mark-room. Blue must also keep clear (because she is to windward).

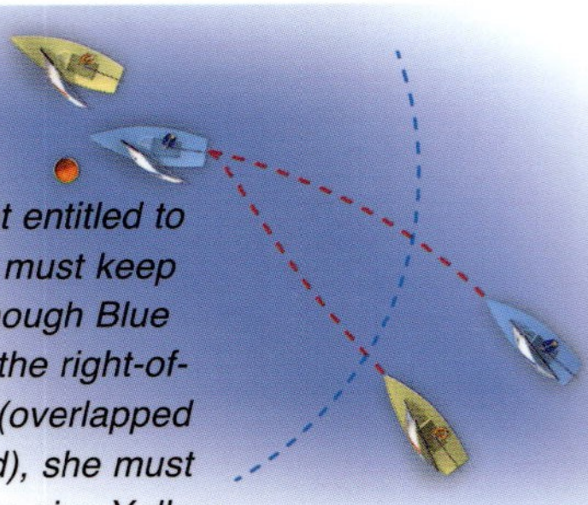

Blue is not entitled to room and must keep clear. Although Blue becomes the right-of-way boat (overlapped to leeward), she must continue to give Yellow mark room.

RULE 18.2

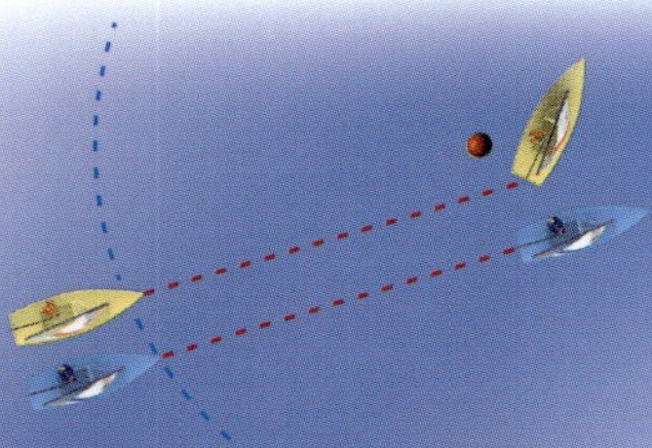

Yellow, overlapped inside, is entitled to room to luff up to head to wind (her proper course to round the mark). When she passes head to wind she is no longer entitled to mark-room and becomes the keep-clear boat while tacking.

Definitions Mark-Room & Proper Course
RULES 18.2(a), 18.2(b) & 13

If a boat is clear ahead when she reaches the zone, the boat clear astern must thereafter give mark-room unless the clear-ahead boat passes head to wind.

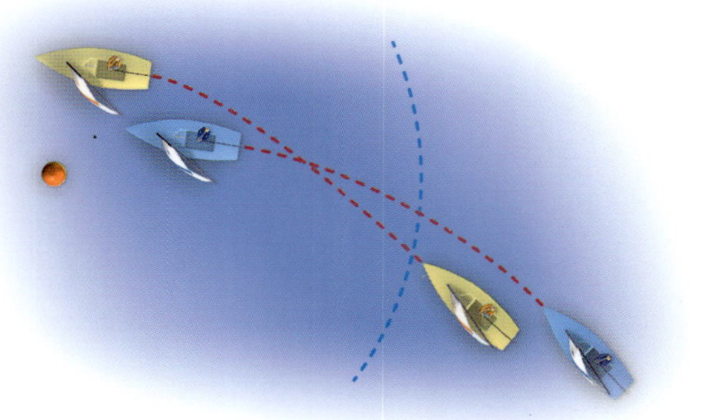

Blue must keep clear and then give Yellow the room she needs to be able to round the mark.

RULE 18.2(a)

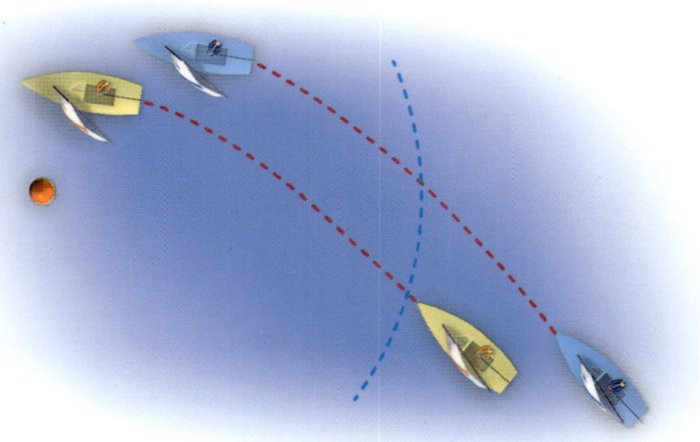

Blue must keep clear and give mark-room.

RULES 11 & 18.2(a)

There is an exception at a starting mark. Yellow has no right to mark-room and must keep clear.

RULE Section C Preamble

DOUBT ABOUT AN OVERLAP

If there is reasonable doubt that a boat obtained or broke an overlap in time, it shall be presumed that she did not. In other words, the situation at the zone is resolved in favour of the situation before the zone when there was no doubt.

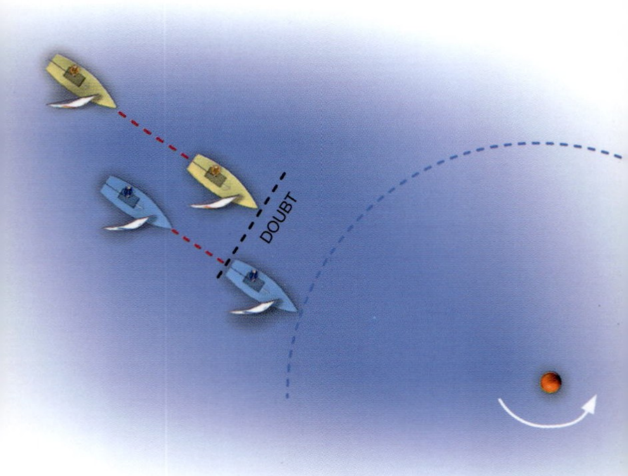

There was no overlap before the zone so when there is doubt at the zone, Yellow must keep clear and give Blue mark-room.

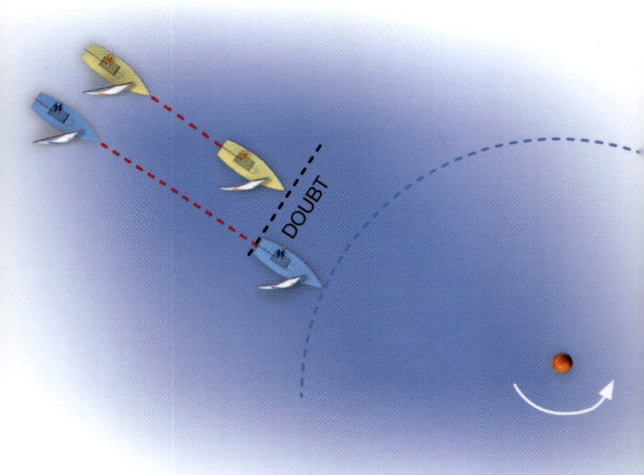

Here Yellow was overlapped before the zone so when there is doubt at the zone, Yellow has the right to mark-room.

RULE 18.2(e)

ROOM TO TACK AT AN OBSTRUCTION

When you are close-hauled (or above) and need to tack to avoid an obstruction, but cannot tack and avoid another boat (to windward or astern), you may hail 'Room to tack' (you must use those words). Before tacking you must give the hailed boat time to respond. The hailed boat must either tack as soon as possible, in which case you must also tack as soon as you have room, or she must reply 'You tack', in which case you must immediately tack and she must give you room. This rule doesn't apply at a starting mark surrounded by navigable water when boats are starting.

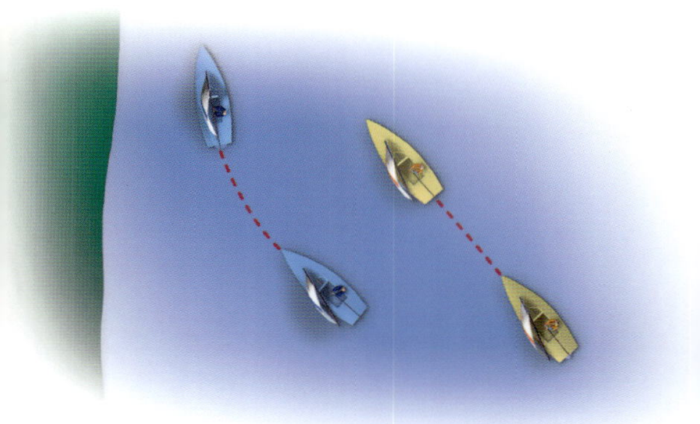

Blue may hail 'room to tack'. Yellow must respond by tacking (or hailing 'You tack' and keeping clear).

RULE 20

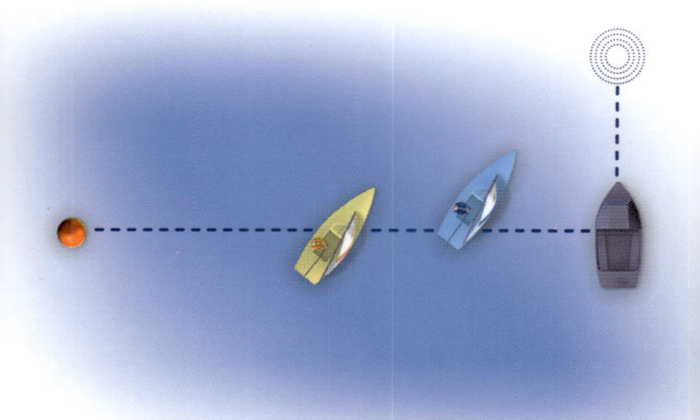

Blue may not hail for room to tack for the anchor line because these boats have just started and have not yet passed the obstruction.

RULE Section C Preamble

SAILING ALONG A CONTINUING OBSTRUCTION (E.G. SHORELINE)

A boat clear astern that is required to keep clear, that obtains an inside overlap, is entitled to room to pass between the other boat and the obstruction only if, at the moment the overlap begins, there is room to do so. If there is not, she is not entitled to room and must keep clear.

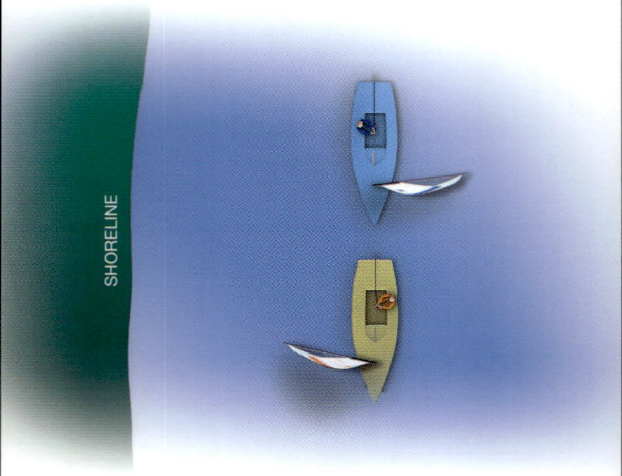

Yellow (on port tack) must keep clear.

RULE 10
Definition Continuing Obstruction

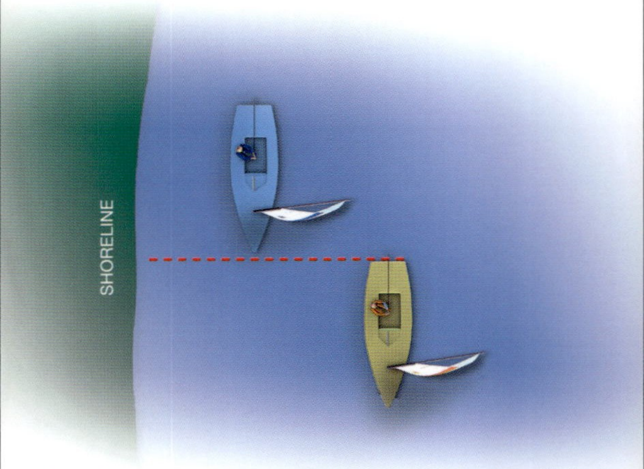

If at the moment the overlap begins, there is sufficient room for Blue to pass between Yellow and the shore, Blue has the right to room. If not, Yellow is not required to give room.

RULE 19.2(c) then RULE 19.2(b)

A LEEWARD BOAT CAN BE AN OBSTRUCTION

Sometimes a right-of-way boat is an obstruction. An outside boat must give an inside boat room unless she has been unable to do so from the moment the overlap was established.

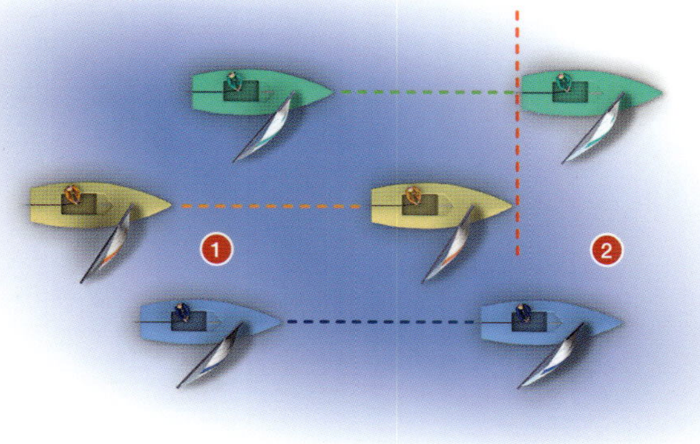

Blue is an obstruction for Yellow and Green. When Yellow establishes an overlap to leeward of Green, Green must give Yellow room to pass between her and the obstruction if she is able to do so from the time the overlap began.

RULE 19.2(b)

A STARBOARD-TACK BOAT CAN BE AN OBSTRUCTION

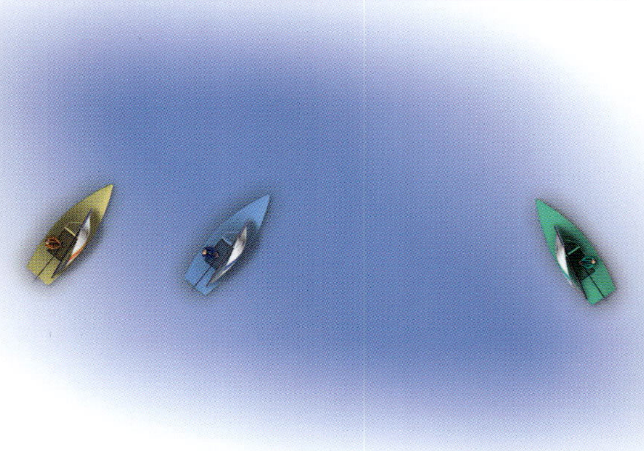

Blue can choose to hail 'room to tack', or bear away to pass astern of Green. If Blue hails, Yellow must respond by tacking or hailing 'you tack' and giving room. Yellow has the right to room between Green and Blue only if Blue chooses to pass astern of Green.

RULES 20 & 19

20. PENALTY TURNS

If you break a 'when boats meet' rule, you may exonerate yourself by sailing clear of other boats as soon as possible and making two turns in the same direction including two tacks and two gybes. If you take a penalty at or near the finishing line, it doesn't matter where you take the penalty but your hull must be completely on the course side of the line before you can finish.

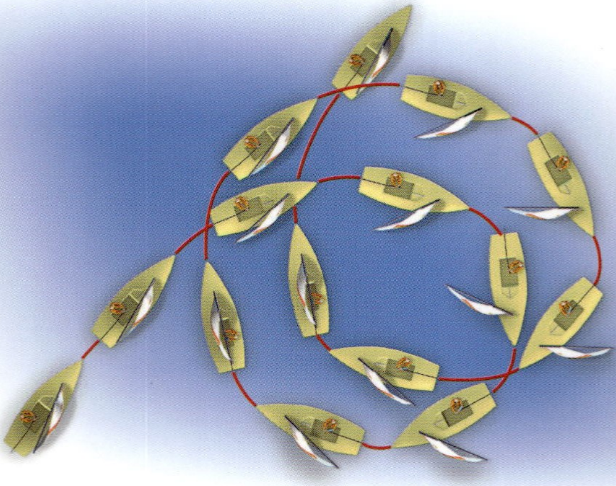

If your boat (or crew or equipment) touches a mark, you may exonerate yourself by sailing clear of other boats as soon as possible and making one turn including a tack and a gybe.

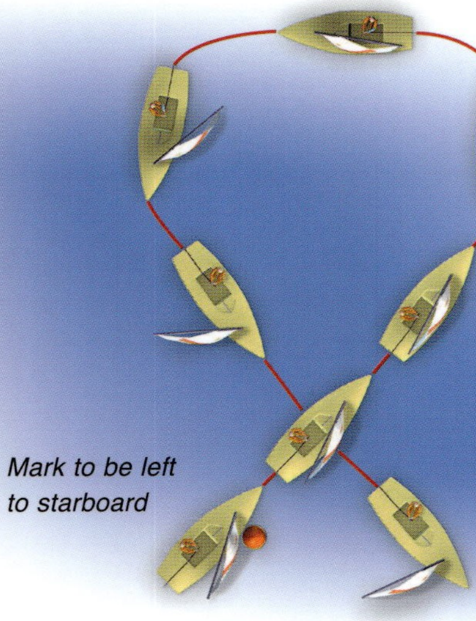

RULES 44.1 & 44.2

The standard starting signalling sequence is:

5 minutes* before the start	Warning signal (the relevant class flag) displayed
4 minutes before the start	Preparatory signal (see below) displayed
1 minute before the start	Preparatory signal removed
Start	Class flag removed

**Sometimes the sailing instructions increase this, for example to 10 minutes*

Preparatory signals

P No penalty for being on the course side of the starting line in the final minute before the starting signal but, of course, you must get back behind the line, and start.

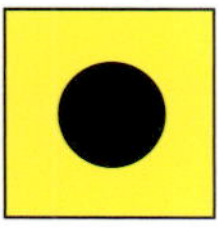

I If over the line in the final minute, you must sail across a line extension (either end of the starting line) from the course side before starting.

Z 20% penalty if in the triangle formed by the line and the first mark in the final minute. You must also go back behind the line and start.

U Disqualified if in the triangle in the final minute, but you can compete if the race is re-sailed.

Black Disqualified if in the triangle in the final minute. You cannot compete if the race is re-sailed.

Each visual signal is accompanied by a sound signal.

RULES OF PART 3

Recall signals

X If any part of a boat's hull is on the course side of the starting line at the start, the race committee will display flag X and make an additional sound signal.

First Substitute If lots of boats are over and the race committee cannot identify them, there may be a general recall. The race committee displays the First Substitute with two extra sound signals.

22. VISUAL SIGNALS

Postponement signals

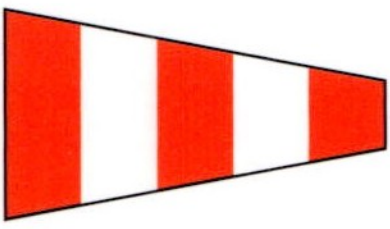

AP The race committee might postpone the race by displaying flag AP (the 'answering pennant') with two sound signals. When it is removed (with a sound signal) the warning signal will be in one minute.

H If flag AP is displayed with flag H it means the next signals will be displayed ashore – so you can go **Home**.

A If flag AP is displayed with flag A it means races are postponed to **Another** day.

Other signals on a Committee boat

Y Wear a personal flotation device.

N Race is abandoned.

Blue The staff displaying this flag is one end of the finishing line.

Orange The staff displaying this flag is one end of the starting line.

M This replaces a missing mark.

C Position of next mark has been changed. Next leg changed to: Port ■ Starboard ▲

S The course has been shortened (finish between the nearby mark and this flag or through the gate).

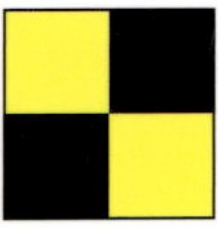

L Come within hail or follow me (or, if displayed ashore, new sailing instruction posted).

V Monitor the race committee communication channel for search & rescue instructions.

PROTESTING

If you see what you think is a boat breaking a rule, you may protest. You must hail 'Protest' immediately if the boat is close enough to hear. If not, you must inform her as soon as possible.

Unless your hull length is 6 metres or less, you must put up a red flag as soon as reasonably possible and leave it conspicuously displayed for the remainder of the race. When you come ashore you must lodge your protest in writing, within a time limit, to the protest committee. You don't have to go ahead with it if you change your mind. If you have actually lodged it, you can ask to withdraw it. Don't be reluctant to protest if you feel aggrieved.

RULES 60.1, 60.2, 60.3 & 60.4

REQUESTING REDRESS

If, through no fault of your own, your finishing position has been, or may be, made significantly worse by an improper action or omission of the race committee, or by being physically damaged by another boat that has broken a rule, you may be able to get redress (for example by being given points for an estimated finishing position). You need to apply in writing to the protest committee.

RULES 61.1 & 61.2

REQUESTING A RE-OPENING

If you can convince the protest committee that it may have made an error, or significant new evidence becomes available, a hearing can be re-opened.

RULE 63.7

APPEALING

At most events you can appeal to your National Authority a decision of a protest committee, but only on a question of rules interpretation or procedures, not on the facts decided by the protest committee.

RULE 70.1

For an in depth discussion,
plus the Rules and Appendices in full, see

The Rules in Practice 2025-2028

by Bryan Willis

Bryan Willis is a leading authority on the rules of yacht and dinghy racing. He has been chairman of the jury and chief umpire for some of the most prestigious sailing events in the world. He served on the International Sailing Federation (now World Sailing) Racing Rules Committee for over 25 years.

FERNHURST BOOKS

Reprinted in 2025 by Fernhurst Books Limited

Published in 2024 by Fernhurst Books Limited
The Windmill, Mill Lane, Harbury, Leamington Spa, CV33 9PH, UK.
Tel: +44 (0) 1926 337488 | www.fernhurstbooks.com

e available in ebook

British Library Cataloguing in Publication Data
A catalogue record for this book is available from the British Library
ISBN 9781912621743

Designed by PPL & Rachel Atkins
Printed in India by Thomson Press India Ltd.

ISBN 9781912621743

£8.99 / US $13.60 / EUR €10.40